Classica Quantum:

A Complete Guide to the Evolution of Computers

By
Naveen Patidar

Contents

Dear Reader,

Thank you for choosing *Classical to Quantum: A Complete Guide to the Evolution of Computers*. This book is the result of deep research and a passion for exploring how computing has transformed from mechanical devices to the quantum era. Your insights and feedback are invaluable in refining future editions and ensuring this book serves as a valuable resource for all readers.

If you find this book informative, engaging, or thought-provoking, I would greatly appreciate it if you could share your thoughts in a review. Your review not only helps other readers but also supports the ongoing journey of knowledge sharing.

Happy reading!

Naveen Patidar

Introduction

From ancient mechanical devices to the cutting-edge world of quantum computing, the journey of computers has been nothing short of extraordinary. *Classical to Quantum: A Complete Guide to the Evolution of Computers* takes you through this incredible transformation, exploring the milestones that shaped the technology we rely on today and the future possibilities that quantum computing promises.

The book begins with one of the earliest known computing devices, the Antikythera Mechanism, a testament to the ingenuity of ancient civilizations. From there, we move through the groundbreaking contributions of Blaise Pascal, Gottfried Wilhelm Leibniz, and Charles Babbage, whose mechanical designs laid the foundation for modern computing. The introduction of vacuum tubes marked the rise of electronic computers, but it was the invention of the transistor at Bell Labs and later the integrated circuit that revolutionized computing, shrinking machines from room-sized behemoths to devices that fit in our pockets.

As computers became more powerful with microprocessors, a new paradigm emerged one that defies the very principles of classical physics. Richard Feynman's vision and the double-slit experiment opened the door to a world where information is processed in ways previously unimaginable. The principles of quantum mechanics introduced ideas such as superposition, quantum decoherence, and error correction, pushing the boundaries of computation.

Today, quantum computing is no longer theoretical; companies like Google are making breakthroughs with innovations such as the Willow Chip. But the real power of quantum computing lies in its applications revolutionizing drug discovery, disease treatment, artificial intelligence, space exploration, and even the fundamental laws of physics and mathematics. This book serves as a guide to understanding this technological evolution.

The Antikythera Mechanism: The First Computer

Imagine an ancient shipwreck, lying untouched at the bottom of the sea for over 2,000 years. Among the scattered treasures and broken artifacts, divers discover a mysterious lump of corroded bronze and wood. At first glance, it looks like nothing more than a decayed relic, but as scientists study it over the decades, they uncover something extraordinary a mechanical device so advanced that it challenges everything we thought we knew about ancient technology. This is the **Antikythera Mechanism**, often referred to as the world's first analog computer.

In 1900, a group of Greek sponge divers set out on a routine expedition near the tiny island of Antikythera, located between mainland Greece and Crete.

When one of them dove deep into the crystal-clear waters, he stumbled upon something unexpected an ancient shipwreck filled with statues, pottery, and jewelry. It was a discovery that would captivate archaeologists for decades.

Amidst the treasures lay a seemingly insignificant, corroded chunk of bronze and wood. It was taken to the National Archaeological Museum of Athens, where it remained largely ignored for years. Only in 1902 did archaeologist Valerios Stais notice something peculiar gears embedded within the corroded metal. This was not just another ancient artifact; it was a complex mechanism with an unknown purpose.

As researchers examined the fragments, they realized they were looking at a device with an intricate system of gears, dials, and inscriptions. Over the next century, technological advancements such as X-ray imaging allowed scientists to peer inside the corroded mass and reconstruct the mechanism's original design.

The Antikythera Mechanism consists of at least **30 interlocking bronze gears**, encased in a wooden box the size of a shoebox.

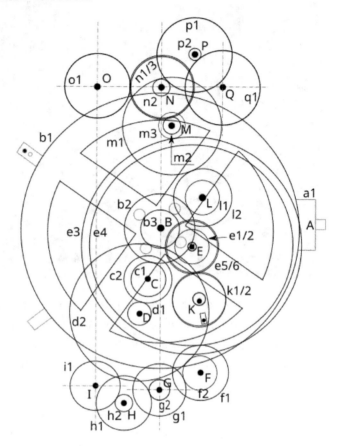

It features dials on the front and back, engraved with Greek inscriptions that provided instructions for its use. The device is now believed to have been used to:

- Predict solar and lunar eclipses with remarkable accuracy.
- Track the movements of the Sun, Moon, and planets according to ancient Greek astronomical models.
- Determine the dates of the Olympic Games, which were held every four years.
- Display the lunar calendar and the phases of the Moon.

Essentially, it was an astronomical calculator, capable of simulating the movements of celestial bodies centuries before the development of modern mechanical clocks.

One of the most debated questions surrounding the Antikythera Mechanism is: **Who built it?**

While no definitive answer exists, historians believe the device was created around **150–100 BCE**, during the Hellenistic period. The level of craftsmanship suggests it was made by Greek scientists, possibly connected to the legendary polymath **Archimedes of Syracuse** or the astronomers of **Rhodes and Alexandria** two ancient hubs of scientific knowledge.

The Greek astronomer **Hipparchus** (c. 190–120 BCE), who developed early theories on the movement of celestial bodies, is often considered a possible influence. The precision of the mechanism aligns with his groundbreaking work on the Moon's motion, further supporting the idea that it was built by astronomers with extensive knowledge of planetary cycles.

What makes the Antikythera Mechanism so astonishing is that nothing of comparable complexity was seen again until the 14th century, when European clockmakers began developing astronomical timepieces. This means there was a gap of over 1,500 years between the Antikythera Mechanism and similar devices.

Historians believe the knowledge required to build such mechanisms may have been lost due to the decline of Greek and Roman civilizations. The destruction of the Library of Alexandria and centuries of turmoil might have erased much of the scientific progress made during antiquity. The rediscovery of mechanical engineering during the Renaissance may have been, in part, a reinvention of lost Greek knowledge.

In the last few decades, the Antikythera Mechanism has undergone extensive study using high-resolution X-ray tomography, 3D modeling, and other advanced technologies.

Some key discoveries include:

Hidden Inscriptions: Over **3,500 characters** of Greek text were found inside the device, serving as an instruction manual. **New Gears Identified:** Scientists now believe the mechanism was even more complex than previously thought, possibly including additional planetary tracking functions. **Mathematical Precision:** The gear ratios align with known ancient Greek astronomical theories, confirming the sophistication of the device's creators.

Why Is the Antikythera Mechanism Called a Computer?

For many people, the word "computer" brings to mind modern devices laptops, smartphones, or even powerful supercomputers crunching vast amounts of data. But what if I told you that a computer existed more than 2,000 years ago, built by ancient Greek engineers? This is precisely why the Antikythera Mechanism is often referred to as the world's first analog computer even though it looks nothing like the digital machines we use today.

So, what exactly makes the Antikythera Mechanism a computer? And if it is a computer, does that mean even a simple calculator falls under the same definition? To answer this, we need to explore the fundamental meaning of what a computer actually is.

The word computer originates from the Latin word *computare*, meaning "to calculate" or "to count." Before electronic computers were invented, the term referred to people yes, human computers who performed complex calculations manually.

In its simplest form, a computer is any device that processes input, follows a set of instructions (an algorithm), and produces an output. It doesn't necessarily have to be electronic. A mechanical system that follows pre-defined rules to compute an answer is still a computer by definition.

This broad definition applies to:

Digital Computers (like modern PCs and smartphones)
Analog Computers (like the Antikythera Mechanism)
Simple Calculators (which also perform computations based on inputs)

Now, let's break this down further.

The Antikythera Mechanism, discovered in a shipwreck off the coast of Greece, is a complex device made of bronze gears that tracked the movements of celestial bodies. Scientists believe it was used to predict solar and lunar eclipses, model planetary positions, and even keep track of the Olympic Games calendar.

But why is it called a computer?

It Processes Input and Produces an Output

The user would set a dial to a specific date (input), and the mechanism would calculate and display astronomical positions and eclipse predictions (output).

It Uses a Mechanical Algorithm

Inside the device, a series of gears worked together to perform calculations based on mathematical models of the solar system. This is very similar to how modern computers follow algorithms to process data.

It Automates Complex Calculations

Instead of requiring a person to manually track planetary movements, the mechanism automated the process, making it much faster and more accurate.

For these reasons, historians and scientists classify the Antikythera Mechanism as an early form of a mechanical computer a device that computes astronomical data without human intervention beyond setting the initial parameters.

The Pascaline: Blaise Pascal's Mechanical Calculator (1642)

In the grand timeline of computing history, one of the earliest mechanical devices designed to perform calculations was the **Pascaline**, invented in **1642** by the French mathematician and philosopher **Blaise Pascal**. At just 19 years old, Pascal set out to create a machine that could help his father, a tax collector, perform complex arithmetic more efficiently. The result was one of the world's first mechanical calculators an intricate device that laid the foundation for future advancements in computational machinery.

The **Pascaline**, also known as the **Arithmetic Machine** or the **Numerical Wheel Calculator**, was built to automate addition and subtraction, making it a breakthrough in an era when calculations were done manually using abacuses and written methods. Unlike modern digital calculators, the Pascaline operated entirely on mechanical principles, using a series of interlocking gears and dials to represent numbers and perform calculations.

How the Pascaline Worked

At its core, the Pascaline functioned through a series of rotating wheels, each representing a digit from 0 to 9. The user would input numbers by turning these wheels, which would then engage a system of gears to perform the desired arithmetic operation.

One of the key features of the Pascaline was the **carry mechanism**. This allowed numbers to automatically carry over to the next digit place, similar to how we carry over numbers in handwritten arithmetic. For example, when a wheel moved past 9, it would trigger the adjacent wheel to advance by one unit, just as adding 1 to 99 results in 100. This automation of carrying over was a major innovation, making calculations faster and reducing human error.

The machine was encased in a rectangular brass or wooden box, with small windows displaying the results of calculations. Users operated the device by inserting a stylus into slots corresponding to numbers, rotating the wheels to the desired values, and then reading the output through the display windows.

Example Calculation: 48 + 26

First, set 48 on the Pascaline (turn the tens dial to 4 and the units dial to 8). Next, add 26 by rotating the tens dial two more steps and the units dial six more steps. When the units dial moves from 8 to 9, then 0, it automatically moves the tens dial by one step, making it 7. The result displayed in the windows is 74.

How the Pascaline Performs Subtraction

Since the Pascaline could not subtract directly, it used a trick called "complementary addition." Instead of subtracting, it would add the complement of a number to 10.

Example Calculation: 73 − 28

Since the Pascaline could not subtract directly, it used a trick called "complementary addition." Instead of subtracting, it would add the complement of a number to 10.

First, set 73 on the Pascaline. Instead of subtracting 28, the machine adds the complement of 28 to 100 (which is 72). (100 - 28 = 72) When 73 + 72 = 145, the machine ignores the extra hundred and displays 45, the correct answer.

The Pascaline had six to eight digit dials, meaning it could handle numbers up to the hundreds of thousands an impressive feat for its time. Each dial was connected to a horizontal bar that engaged a gear mechanism. By adjusting the dials, users could add or subtract numbers mechanically without requiring mental calculations.

Pascal designed several variations of the machine, refining its operation and improving its efficiency. However, despite its ingenuity, the Pascaline had limitations:

Only addition and subtraction were possible. Multiplication and division required repeated addition or subtraction.

It was expensive and difficult to manufacture, limiting its widespread adoption.

Users had to be trained to operate it properly, as the mechanism was complex compared to traditional calculation methods.

Gottfried Wilhelm Leibniz and the Step Reckoner

Blaise Pascal's **Pascaline** of 1642 was a remarkable first step in the journey toward mechanical computation. However, it had its limitations it could only handle addition and subtraction, and the user had to manually adjust dials for carrying over numbers. While it eased the burden of calculation, mathematicians and engineers sought to push the boundaries further. Among them was **Gottfried Wilhelm Leibniz**, who took mechanical calculation to the next level with his **Step Reckoner** in 1673.

The evolution of computers is a fascinating journey, marked by the brilliance of inventors who dared to push the limits of mathematics and engineering. Among these pioneers, Gottfried Wilhelm Leibniz, a German polymath of the 17th century, stands out for his groundbreaking contribution to mechanical computation. In **1673**, Leibniz introduced the **Stepped Reckoner**, a mechanical calculator that could perform all four basic arithmetic operations: addition, subtraction, multiplication, and division.

This was a major advancement beyond Blaise Pascal's Pascaline, which could only handle addition and subtraction. Leibniz's Step Reckoner laid the foundation for future calculating machines, influencing generations of inventors who followed.

Leibniz was not just a mathematician; he was a philosopher, scientist, and inventor with an unquenchable thirst for knowledge. He believed that human reasoning, including mathematical calculations, could be automated through mechanical means. Inspired by Pascal's mechanical calculator, Leibniz envisioned a more advanced machine that could handle complex calculations with greater ease and efficiency.

He began working on the design of his **Step Reckoner (or Staffelwalze, in German)** in the 1670s. By 1673, he presented a working prototype to the Royal Society in London, demonstrating how the machine could multiply numbers through repeated addition. His goal was to eliminate the tedious process of manual calculations, making mathematical operations faster and more accurate.

Unlike Pascal's calculator, which relied on a simple system of rotating wheels, Leibniz introduced a new mechanical component the **stepped drum**, or **Leibniz wheel**. This innovation became the backbone of many later mechanical calculators, remaining in use well into the 20th century.

How the Step Reckoner Worked

At its core, the Step Reckoner was designed to mimic the process of manual calculations but in a fully mechanical way. The key element of the machine was the stepped drum, a cylindrical gear with a series of staggered teeth of increasing length.

The machine featured:

A series of dials and levers to input numbers. A movable carriage that adjusted positions to facilitate different operations. A stepped drum mechanism, which engaged different gears based on the input, enabling multiplication and division with fewer steps. A result display window, where users could read the final answer.

For addition and subtraction, the mechanism worked similarly to Pascal's machine: the user set numbers by adjusting dials, and the machine carried over values automatically. But for multiplication, the Step Reckoner used a process of repeated additions, shifting the mechanical carriage to handle different place values. Similarly, for division, it performed repeated subtractions, automating a process that was previously tedious and error-prone.

This ability to perform multiplication and division made the Step Reckoner vastly superior to Pascal's machine, which required users to manually repeat addition or subtraction multiple times to achieve the same result.

Despite its revolutionary design, the Step Reckoner faced technical and practical challenges. One of the main issues was mechanical complexity it was difficult to manufacture with the precision needed for reliable operation. The gears and moving parts often encountered friction and alignment problems, making the machine prone to errors and malfunctions.

Additionally, because of its size and weight, the Step Reckoner was not a practical device for widespread use. Unlike modern calculators, which fit in the palm of a hand, Leibniz's machine was large, cumbersome, and difficult to transport. These limitations meant that, although the concept was groundbreaking, the Step Reckoner did not see commercial success in its time.

Although the Step Reckoner did not achieve widespread use, Leibniz's contributions to computing were far-reaching. His stepped drum mechanism became a fundamental component of many later mechanical calculators, including those developed in the 19th and early 20th centuries. The design principles he introduced paved the way for more refined calculating devices, such as Charles Babbage's Difference Engine and Analytical Engine.

Moreover, Leibniz's influence extended beyond mechanical computation. He was an early advocate of **binary arithmetic**, recognizing that numbers could be represented using just two digits 0 and 1. This insight, though not widely recognized at the time, later became the foundation of modern digital computers. Today, every computer operates on binary logic, a principle that Leibniz foresaw centuries ago.

Charles Babbage and the Dawn of Mechanical Computing

As we journey through the evolution of computing machines, we move from Gottfried Wilhelm Leibniz's groundbreaking work on binary numbers and his Stepped Reckoner to another visionary mind: Charles Babbage. If Leibniz laid the foundation for computational thinking with binary arithmetic, Babbage took it a step further by conceptualizing mechanical machines that could perform complex calculations automatically.

Babbage, often called the **"father of the computer,"** was an English mathematician, engineer, and inventor who lived in the 19th century. His ambitious ideas for mechanized computation led to the development of two significant designs: the **Difference Engine** and the **Analytical Engine**. Though neither was fully completed during his lifetime, they introduced principles that became the basis for modern computing.

The Difference Engine:

The world in which Babbage lived was one that heavily relied on mathematical tables for navigation, engineering, and finance. However, these tables were prone to human errors, as they were calculated and transcribed manually. Babbage, frustrated by these inaccuracies, envisioned a machine that could generate error-free mathematical tables.

In the early 1820s, he began working on the Difference Engine, a mechanical device designed to calculate polynomial functions using the method of finite differences. This method allowed complex calculations to be broken down into simple repetitive additions, making them feasible for a machine to handle.

The Difference Engine was composed of thousands of mechanical parts, including gears, levers, and columns.

It was intended to automatically compute and print mathematical tables, eliminating human mistakes. The British government recognized its potential and funded the project, but as the machine became more complex, the costs skyrocketed. Babbage's perfectionism led him to redesign the machine multiple times, making it even more intricate. By the early 1830s, the project was abandoned due to financial constraints and technical difficulties.

Though the original Difference Engine was never completed, a fully functional version was later built in 1991 using Babbage's original designs. This demonstrated that his concept was indeed feasible and that his mechanical computing vision was well ahead of its time.

The Analytical Engine:

While working on the Difference Engine, Babbage realized that a more powerful machine could be built one that could perform not just specific calculations but any kind of mathematical computation. This led to the conception of the

Analytical Engine, which was, in many ways, the first design of a general-purpose computer.

The Analytical Engine, designed in the 1830s and 1840s, was a massive leap forward. Unlike the Difference Engine, which was limited to one type of computation, the Analytical Engine was designed to be **programmable**. It had several key components that closely resemble modern computers:

The Store: This acted as the memory of the machine, where numbers and intermediate results were stored. It could hold up to 1,000 numbers of 40 digits each, making it far more sophisticated than previous calculating machines.

The Mill: This was essentially the processing unit (akin to today's CPU), where mathematical operations were carried out.

The Input and Output Mechanisms: The machine was designed to use punched cards (inspired by the Jacquard loom) to input instructions and receive results, much like how early 20th-century computers functioned.

Conditional Branching and Loops: One of the most remarkable aspects of the Analytical Engine was its ability to make decisions based on the results of calculations. This concept, which we now call conditional branching, is a core feature of modern programming.

The Control Unit: The machine had a mechanism to sequence instructions, making it capable of executing a series of calculations autonomously without manual intervention.

Ada Lovelace: The First Programmer

Babbage's work might have remained purely theoretical if not for Ada Lovelace, an English mathematician and writer who collaborated with him. She saw the full potential of the Analytical Engine, realizing that it could do much more than just arithmetic it could be programmed to perform a sequence of operations.

In 1843, she translated and expanded upon an article written about the Analytical Engine, adding her own extensive notes. Within these notes, she wrote what is considered the **first algorithm** designed for a machine, effectively making her the world's first computer programmer. She predicted that such a machine could one day manipulate symbols, compose music, and even create art ideas that were far ahead of her time.

The Edison Effect

Continuing from Charles Babbage's groundbreaking contributions to computational machines, we now move forward to another visionary who played a crucial role in shaping the future of computing Thomas Edison.

While Edison is most famously known for inventing the practical incandescent light bulb, his contributions to the development of computing systems are often overlooked.

One of Edison's key contributions was the refinement of the thermionic emission effect, often referred to as the Edison Effect. This principle, where electrons flow from a heated filament to a positively charged plate, later became discoveries came in 1883 while experimenting with his incandescent light bulbs. He noticed that when a metal plate was placed inside the bulb, a mysterious electrical current seemed to flow through the vacuum from the heated filament to the plate. Over time, he observed that one side of the bulb's interior became coated with a brownish layer. This phenomenon, later called the " **the thermionic emission effect,"** was the first recorded instance of thermionic emission the principle that would become the basis for vacuum tube technology. Vacuum tubes were crucial in the first generation of computers, as they functioned as switches and amplifiers, allowing machines to process binary data at unprecedented speeds.

Before transistors revolutionized computing in the mid-20th century, vacuum tubes played the same role as modern semiconductor switches. In early computers like the ENIAC (Electronic Numerical Integrator and Computer), thousands of vacuum tubes were used to perform calculations by switching electrical currents on and off, effectively representing the 0s and 1s of binary code. This ability to control electrical currents with vacuum tubes was essential for early computation, and it all stemmed from Edison's pioneering work in electrical science. The Edison Effect revealed something crucial: electrons could move freely in a vacuum under the right conditions. This was a groundbreaking realization because it provided insight into how electricity could be controlled and manipulated to perform different tasks. Edison had essentially discovered a way to direct the flow of current without direct contact between components, paving the way for electronic circuits.

Beyond the vacuum tube, Edison's establishment of electrical power infrastructure also indirectly supported the growth of computing. His work in setting up electric power grids made it possible for computers and other electronic devices to be powered reliably. The widespread availability of electrical power was a crucial factor in enabling the technological advancements that led to modern computing Though Edison himself did not fully explore the implications of his discovery, other scientists later built upon it. British physicist **John Ambrose Fleming** used the Edison Effect to develop the first vacuum tube diode in 1904, which could control the flow of electricity in one direction. This principle became the foundation of electronic circuits and, eventually, early computers.

Thus, while Thomas Edison was not directly involved in designing or conceptualizing computers, his innovations in electricity and vacuum tube technology played an indispensable role in shaping early electronic computers. His contributions bridged the gap between mechanical computing machines like Babbage's Analytical Engine and the fully electronic computers that would emerge in the 20th century. The ability to control electric current was a massive leap forward in computing history. Early computers relied on thousands of vacuum tubes acting as electronic switches, turning on and off to represent the binary 0s and 1s that form the basis of all modern computing. Without Edison's discoveries, the evolution of computers as we know them today might have followed a very different path accidental discovery of the Edison Effect, the development of these electronic circuits might have been significantly delayed.

Beyond vacuum tubes, Edison's work in establishing electrical power infrastructure also played a critical role in computing's evolution. His efforts in developing power generation, transmission, and distribution systems ensured that electronic devices, including computers, could function efficiently. The spread of electrical power networks enabled scientists and engineers to experiment with electrical circuits, leading to advancements in telecommunications, radio, and, eventually, computing.

Thus, Thomas Edison's contributions to computing were not just about the light bulb. His discoveries about electric current, thermionic emission, and vacuum tube principles were vital in setting the stage for the first electronic computers. His work bridged the gap between mechanical computing machines like Babbage's Analytical Engine and the electronic revolution that followed. Edison didn't invent the computer, but without his discoveries, the journey toward digital computing would have taken a very different path.

Rise of Vacuum Tube Computing

Continuing from Thomas Edison's discovery of the Edison Effect, it is essential to explore how this phenomenon evolved into vacuum tube technology and, subsequently, early computers. The vacuum tube, also known as a **thermionic valve,** became the backbone of electronic circuits for the first computing machines.

A vacuum tube is essentially an electric circuit enclosed in a glass tube with a vacuum inside. It consists of four key components: **a metal plate (anode), a grid, a heater (filament),** and **glass walls.** Here's how it works:

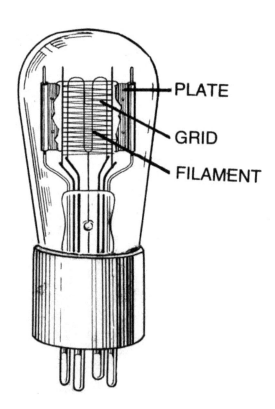

When an electric current passes through the filament, it heats up and emits electrons. This process is based on thermionic emission, the principle first observed in Edison's bulbs.

Positioned inside the vacuum tube, the metal plate attracts the free electrons released by the heated filament. Placed between the filament and the anode, the grid acts as a gatekeeper, regulating the flow of electrons. By applying different voltages, the grid can control whether electrons reach the plate or not, effectively acting as a switch or an amplifier. The glass enclosure maintains a vacuum, preventing air molecules from interfering with the free movement of electrons.

This basic mechanism allowed vacuum tubes to be used as electronic switches, replacing mechanical components in computing devices. The ability to control electrical flow digitally (on and off states) enabled the representation of binary code 0s and 1s which is the foundation of modern computing.

With the understanding of vacuum tubes, engineers started integrating them into large computing machines. Early computers like the ENIAC (Electronic Numerical Integrator and Computer) used thousands of vacuum tubes to perform calculations. These vacuum tubes essentially acted as electronic switches, replacing the mechanical gears of earlier computing devices.

At this stage, computers operated using glowing bulbs inside vacuum tubes, making them resemble large, glowing cabinets. These machines could process information much faster than mechanical computers, but they still had several limitations.

Despite their groundbreaking advancements, vacuum tube-based computers had significant drawbacks:

Constantly Replacing Bulbs: The filament inside vacuum tubes would burn out over time, requiring frequent replacements. Since early computers used thousands of these tubes, maintenance was a significant issue.

Heat Generation: The continuous operation of vacuum tubes produced immense heat, leading to overheating problems. Special cooling systems were required to prevent the computers from failing.

Size and Power Consumption: Early computers filled entire rooms, consuming vast amounts of electricity. The complexity of wiring thousands of vacuum tubes made these machines bulky and inefficient.

The Birth of the Transistor at Bell Labs

After the breakthroughs of Thomas Edison and the vacuum tube era, the next major leap in computing technology took place in 1947 at Bell Labs. Three brilliant physicists John Bardeen, Walter Brattain, and William Shockley conducted experiments that would forever change the course of technological development. Their work led to the invention of the transistor, a revolutionary device that would replace bulky, power-hungry vacuum tubes and set the stage for modern electronic computing.

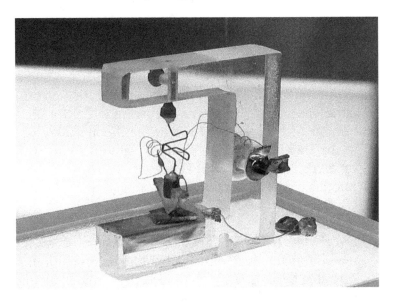

During the 1940s, vacuum tubes were the backbone of electronic circuits. However, they had significant limitations, such as frequent failure, excessive heat generation, and enormous power consumption. Scientists at Bell Labs were determined to find a more efficient alternative.

Bardeen, Brattain, and Shockley focused on a material called **germanium**, a semiconductor that had unique electrical properties. In December 1947, they successfully created the first working transistor using germanium. This tiny device could amplify electrical signals and act as a switch just like a vacuum tube but it was significantly smaller, more reliable, and required far less power.

Although germanium transistors were a breakthrough, they had their own limitations. Germanium was highly temperature-sensitive, and its performance degraded when exposed to high heat. Scientists soon turned their attention to **silicon**, another semiconductor material that was more stable, abundant, and capable of operating under extreme conditions.

By the 1950s, silicon had become the preferred material for making transistors. The shift to silicon was a game-changer, as it paved the way for the creation of integrated circuits and microchips, which are the foundation of all modern computers.

While silicon transistors were becoming the standard, a parallel transformation was occurring in California. Before it became the tech hub of the world, Silicon Valley was known as the **Valley of Heart's Delight**, famous for its fruit orchards and agriculture. However, the region soon evolved into the center of semiconductor innovation, giving birth to what we now call **Silicon Valley**.

So why the name Silicon Valley? The answer lies in the material that powered the technological revolution: **silicon**. The area became home to pioneering semiconductor companies, making it the heart of the microelectronics industry.

One of the key factors in the rise of Silicon Valley was **Stanford University**. The university encouraged its students and faculty to engage in technological innovation, offering land leases to startups and companies. This initiative led to the establishment of early tech giants such as **Hewlett-Packard (HP)**, which started as a small company in a garage and later became a global leader in computing technology.

During the 1950s and 1960s, several companies emerged in the region, driving the semiconductor industry forward. Some of the most influential companies included:

Fairchild Semiconductor: Founded by eight brilliant engineers, including Robert Noyce and Gordon Moore, Fairchild played a crucial role in the development of silicon transistors and integrated circuits.

IBM and Honeywell: These companies were among the first to develop large-scale computing systems, utilizing the new transistor technology.

Intel and AMD: In the late 1960s, former Fairchild engineers went on to establish **Intel** and **AMD**, two companies that would become giants in the microprocessor industry.

By the 1970s, Silicon Valley had become the epicenter of the computer revolution. With semiconductor companies, computer manufacturers, and research institutions all concentrated in one region, innovation thrived. Over time, this ecosystem expanded beyond semiconductors to include software, networking, and internet-based technologies.

The name **Silicon Valley** has since become synonymous with technology and innovation, but its origins are deeply rooted in the semiconductor industry. Without the development of silicon-based transistors, the modern computer industry would not exist.

This transition from germanium to silicon, from vacuum tubes to transistors, and from farmland to a global tech hub represents one of the most remarkable transformations in history. It set the stage for the computers we use today.

The Invention of the Integrated Circuit

Following the establishment of Silicon Valley, the advancement of computer technology didn't stop it took another massive leap forward. While transistors had replaced bulky vacuum tubes and significantly reduced the size and power consumption of computers, there was still a problem.

Initially, early semiconductor computers still relied on thousands of individual transistors, which needed to be connected using wires. This meant that computers still looked like a tangled mess of circuitry, even though they were much smaller than their vacuum-tube predecessors. The size of the computers had only been reduced by around 30-40% because all the tiny semiconductor components had to be manually connected with wires.

This complexity made computers difficult to manufacture, expensive to maintain, and prone to failure. Just like in the vacuum tube era, if one transistor or wire failed, an entire section of the computer could stop working. Engineers knew that while transistors were revolutionary, they still weren't the perfect solution. They needed a way to reduce the number of connections, simplify the design, and further shrink the size of computers.

The breakthrough came in 1958 when **Jack Kilby,** an engineer at Texas Instruments, introduced the concept of the **integrated circuit (IC).** Instead of using separate transistors and wiring them together, Kilby developed a way to build multiple transistors directly onto a single piece of semiconductor material. This eliminated the need for extensive wiring, drastically reducing size, cost, and energy consumption.

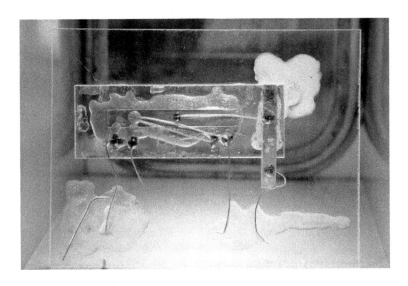

Kilby's first prototype of the integrated circuit was made using germanium, but soon, scientists and engineers realized that **silicon** was an even better material for mass production. Silicon was more abundant, more stable, and could handle higher temperatures without degrading. This led to the rapid adoption of silicon-based integrated circuits, further propelling the computer revolution.

The introduction of integrated circuits changed everything. Suddenly, engineers could pack thousands or even millions of transistors onto a single chip.

The Era of Microprocessors: A Revolution in Computing

After the invention of integrated circuits (ICs), computers became smaller, faster, and more energy-efficient. However, they were still not truly compact. Early ICs connected multiple semiconductor components, but they still required numerous individual connections through wiring. This meant that, despite the progress, computers were still about the size of a mini-fridge. The real breakthrough was yet to come the microprocessor.

In 1970, Intel made history by finalizing the design of the world's first commercial microprocessor, the **Intel 4004**. This invention changed everything. The idea was revolutionary what if an entire computer circuit, with all its processing power, could fit onto a single small chip? That was the power of the microprocessor.

A microprocessor is essentially a complete computer brain on a single silicon chip. Unlike earlier integrated circuits, which required multiple components wired together, a microprocessor integrated all essential computing functions onto one chip. This included:

- Electronic switches to control the flow of electricity.
- An arithmetic logic unit (ALU) to perform calculations.
- Integrated memory for temporary data storage.
- Input-output control circuits to manage communication with external devices.

In 1971, Intel introduced the **Intel 4004**, the first commercially available microprocessor. This tiny chip contained 2,300 transistors and operated at a clock speed of 740 kHz an incredible feat at the time. Before this, a computer with similar computing power would have taken up an entire room. Now, for the first time, processing power was compact enough to fit in the palm of a hand.

The impact was enormous. Before microprocessors, computers were large, expensive machines, accessible only to big corporations and research institutions. But with microprocessors, computers became affordable, paving the way for personal computing.

Intel co-founder **Gordon Moore** made a bold prediction in 1965, which later became known as **Moore's Law**. He observed that the number of transistors in a microprocessor was doubling approximately every two years, leading to exponential increases in computing power. This meant that computers would continue to get smaller, cheaper, and more powerful over time.

Moore's Law wasn't just an observation it became a guiding principle for the semiconductor industry. Companies pushed their research and development efforts to keep up with this trend, making rapid technological advancements possible.

After the Intel 4004, the race to develop better microprocessors began. Each generation brought significant improvements:

Intel 8008 (1972): An improved 8-bit processor, capable of handling more complex instructions.

Intel 8080 (1974): One of the most influential microprocessors, used in early personal computers.

Intel 8086 (1978): The first 16-bit processor, which laid the foundation for modern PC architecture.

Intel 80286, 80386, and beyond: These processors brought more speed, memory capacity, and better multitasking abilities.

By the late 1980s and early 1990s, microprocessors had become the heart of personal computers, gaming consoles, and even embedded systems like calculators and industrial machines.

The advancements in microprocessors led to the explosion of the **personal computer (PC) industry**. Companies like IBM, Apple, and Microsoft took advantage of this technology to build affordable computers for home and office use.

IBM's first personal computer (1981) was powered by an Intel 8088 microprocessor.

Apple's Macintosh (1984) used Motorola's 68000 processor and revolutionized user-friendly computing with its graphical user interface (GUI).

Microsoft's MS-DOS and Windows leveraged Intel's growing microprocessor power, shaping the software industry.

While Intel led the early microprocessor industry, competitors soon emerged.

AMD (Advanced Micro Devices) became a major competitor, producing high-performance processors for both personal and enterprise computers.

ARM (Acorn RISC Machine) developed energy-efficient microprocessors that would later dominate mobile and embedded systems.

Today, microprocessors are not just in computers but in nearly every electronic device smartphones, smart TVs, cars, and even household appliances. The evolution from room-sized computers to pocket-sized smartphones is all thanks to the microprocessor.

The invention of the microprocessor in 1971 was a turning point in the evolution of computers. Intel's 4004 microprocessor, the first of its kind, packed all the core functions of a computer arithmetic, memory, and control into a single silicon chip. This breakthrough marked the beginning of a new era where computing power could be condensed into small, affordable, and powerful devices.

But how was this level of miniaturization even possible? The answer lay in silicon transistors, the fundamental building blocks of microprocessors. Early transistors were large, but as the years passed, engineers found ways to make them smaller and more efficient.

The first microprocessor, Intel's 4004, contained only 2,300 transistors, each measuring around 10,000 nanometers. To put that into perspective, a human hair is about 80,000 nanometers thick! Over the next few decades, engineers worked tirelessly to shrink transistors, making computers faster, smaller, and more powerful.

Fast forward to today, and the latest Intel processors house more than 1.17 billion transistors, with each transistor measuring just 3 nanometers about the width of 20 atoms. But when transistors shrink to the atomic scale, the pathways (roads) through which electrons travel become so narrow that electrons start "leaking" out due to quantum effects. This leads to errors and circuit malfunctions, making the system unreliable. As transistor density increases, heat generation becomes a major issue. Excessive heat can damage circuits and reduce efficiency. Additionally, at such small scales, **electromagnetic interference** becomes significant, further degrading performance. Some engineers have explored 3D stacking, where transistors are layered vertically instead of just shrinking them. While this approach helps improve performance for now, it is not an infinite solution. At some point, even 3D stacking will face thermal and efficiency bottlenecks. Due to these limitations, **Moore's Law**, which predicted that the number of transistors on a chip would double every two years, is now slowing down. Instead of doubling every 2 years, it's now taking around 4 years or more. This suggests that the era of exponential growth in computing power is coming to an end.

Since the transition from mechanical to electronic computers in the 1880s, our processing power has increased by millions of times, and computer sizes have shrunk exponentially. This revolution happened because we harnessed the principles of electronics. But is there an even more fundamental principle that could take us beyond the limits of modern computing? The answer lies in the mysterious and counterintuitive world of **quantum mechanics**.

As we journey deeper into the evolution of computers, one thing becomes clear every major leap in computing has been driven by a fundamental shift in our understanding of the physical world. From the era of vacuum tubes to transistors, and then to microprocessors, our ability to manipulate electrons and encode information has taken us from room-sized computers to pocket-sized supercomputers. But what if there were a way to harness an even deeper law of nature? What if we could exploit the very fabric of reality itself quantum mechanics?

Richard Feynman's Vision

The story of quantum computing begins with one of the most brilliant minds of the 20th century: Richard Feynman. In 1981, during a lecture at the Massachusetts Institute of Technology titled *Simulating Physics with Computers*.

Feynman made a profound observation. He pointed out that nature itself operates under the laws of quantum mechanics, where particles like electrons, atoms, and molecules behave in ways that are completely unintuitive in classical physics. He argued that traditional computers, which rely on binary logic (1s and 0s), would always struggle to fully simulate quantum systems. His famous words from that lecture still echo today:

"Nature is not classical, dammit! And if you want to make a simulation of nature, you'd better make it quantum mechanical."

This statement was more than just a passing remark it was a call to action. If we wanted to build computers capable of simulating the quantum world, we would need to invent machines that obey the very laws of quantum mechanics themselves.

Feynman's ideas laid the foundation for a new type of computing one that wouldn't just process information using bits (1s and 0s) but would instead leverage the strange properties of quantum mechanics. But how would this be possible?

Feynman proposed an idea that would become the backbone of quantum computing: using the quantum states of electrons instead of classical transistors. In classical computers, a transistor is either ON (1) or OFF (0), forming the basis of all computations. Feynman suggested that instead of simple binary states, a quantum system could encode information using electron spin spin up representing 1 and spin down representing 0.

Simply replacing transistors with quantum particles does not automatically enhance a computer's power. The true potential of quantum computing lies in two fundamental principles: **quantum superposition** and **quantum entanglement**. To fully grasp these concepts, it is essential to understand an important experiment **the Double Slit Experiment**.

The double-slit experiment

Imagine you have a vertical plate with two parallel slits in it. If you throw small grains of sand at this plate, you would expect to see two straight lines forming behind it on a screen because the sand grains would pass through the slits in straight paths. This is common sense.

However, if you replace the sand with subatomic particles like electrons or photons and fire them one by one, you won't see just two straight lines on the screen. Instead, you will see multiple lines forming a pattern. This pattern is called an **interference pattern**, which is a characteristic of waves, not particles. Unlike solid particles, waves can interact with themselves and interfere, either amplifying or canceling out.

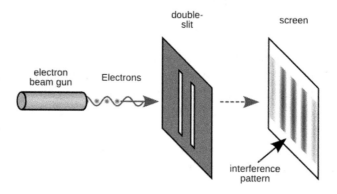

This raises a strange question are these subatomic particles actually waves? We were taught that they are particles, right? The answer is: they are particles, but they also behave like waves. Their movement follows wave-like patterns, which is why this phenomenon is called **wave-particle duality**.

Now, when these particles are fired at the two slits, something strange happens. Even though each particle is an individual object, it acts as if it passes through both slits at the same time, just like a wave would. This phenomenon is called **superposition**, which means the particle exists in multiple states (or places) simultaneously. Imagine if we could use this principle in computing this is exactly what **David Deutsch**, one of the pioneers of quantum computing, proposed in the 1980s.

Back to the experiment once a wave passes through the two slits, it breaks into multiple smaller waves, which then interact with each other. This interaction creates interference. There are two types of interference:

1. **Constructive interference** – When two waves combine in sync, they amplify each other, creating brighter areas on the screen.
2. **Destructive interference** – When two waves cancel each other out, they create dark areas where no particles appear.

Now, look at the bright stripes on the screen behind the slits. These bright areas indicate where the waves have combined (constructive interference), meaning more particles accumulate there.

This experiment teaches us two important things:

1. We cannot pinpoint the exact location of a single particle, but we can predict where it is most likely to appear. The brighter areas on the screen represent higher probabilities of finding a particle.
2. The wave behavior of particles is not deterministic but probabilistic. We cannot say with 100% certainty where a particle will land, but we can use probability to make the best guess.

So, instead of behaving like classical solid objects, these tiny particles behave like waves that follow probability rules. This is one of the fundamental ideas of quantum mechanics.

In 1926, German physicist **Max Born** introduced a formula:

$$P(x,y,z,t_0) = |\Psi(x,y,z,t_0)|^2$$

This equation predicts the probability of finding a particle at a specific location. Essentially, it turned uncertainty into something measurable. This discovery played a crucial role in the development of quantum computers and algorithms.

The double-slit experiment showed that particles could travel through multiple paths simultaneously and later land in regions where they had the highest probability of appearing. This raised an interesting question could we use this principle in computers? Specifically, could we use it to solve problems where there are billions of possible answers, but only one or a few correct ones? For example, breaking high-security encryption codes?

If we break this principle down, the goal of a quantum computer is simple: use the probability and interference effects of quantum mechanics to perform calculations. During processing, quantum waves and their probabilities combine repeatedly. With each step, the system moves closer to the correct answer.

Just like in the double-slit experiment, where wave interactions revealed the probable locations of particles, quantum computers use wave interference to eliminate incorrect answers and amplify the correct one. By canceling out destructive interference and focusing only on the most constructive interference patterns, a quantum computer builds up the correct answer through the interference of billions of quantum waves.

However, to achieve this, we need special algorithms that can mathematically guide this process. The fundamental principle behind quantum computing is to eliminate noise and destructive interference, allowing only constructive interference to amplify the correct solution. This makes quantum computing a revolutionary tool for solving complex problems.

Understanding Classical and Quantum Computers: A Deep Dive

Computers, as we know them today, operate based on classical computing principles. At their core, these machines process and transfer information using classical bits.

To understand the difference between classical and quantum computers, let's first explore how classical computers process information and then compare it to the unique and powerful nature of quantum computing.

In classical computers, information is processed and transmitted through classical bits. These bits serve as the fundamental unit of information and exist in one of two possible states:

0 (zero)
1 (one)

But what exactly determines whether a bit is 0 or 1? The answer lies in **silicon transistors** tiny electronic switches that either allow or block the flow of electricity.

If the transistor is ON, it represents a **1** (high voltage).
If the transistor is OFF, it represents a **0** (low voltage).

These simple on-off states form the basis of every operation in a classical computer. Whether you are typing a document, watching a video, or browsing the internet, all the words, images, videos, and applications on your screen are nothing but long sequences of 0s and 1s.

```
01000100 01000101 01010011 01010000 01001001 01000101 01010010 01010100 01000001 00100000 00100000 01001110
01001111 01010011 00100000 01000101 01010011 01010100 11000011 10000001 01001110 00100000 01001101 01000001
01001110 01001001 01010000 01010101 01001100 01000001 01010010 01000100 01001111 00100000 01000001 00100000
01010011 01010101 00100000 01000001 01001110 01010010 01001111 01010010 01000100 01001111 00100000 01000001
01001100 00100000 01001110 01010111 01001111 01001111 00100000 01000001 01001101 01010000 01001100 01000011
01000001 00100000 01010000 00100000 01010000 01010000 01010010 01000100 01001100 01001001 01000001 00100000
00100000 01000100 01000101 00100000 01010100 01001111 01000100 01000001 01010011 00100000 01001110 01010101
01000101 01010011 01010010 01010010 01001000 01000001 01010011 00100000 01001100 01000101 00100000 01010010
01010100 01000001 01000101 01000101 01010011 01000000 01001001 00100000 01000101 01001100 00100000 01000011
01001111 01001110 01010010 01010100 01010010 01001111 01001100 00100000 01001101 01000001 01001100 01000001
01001001 01001111 01010011 01001111 00100000 01000100 01001100 01001001 01010100 01001111 01000100 01000001
00100000 01001100 00100000 01010101 01001111 01001100 01000100 01001100 01000011 01000001 01001101 11000011
10010011 01001110 00100000 01000001 01010011 11000011 10001101 00100000 01000011 01001111 01001101 01001111
00100000 01010101 01001110 00100000 01000100 01010010 01001110 01010010 01000100 01001101 01001111 01000011
11000011 10010011 01001110 00100000 01000100 01010010 11000011 10000001 01010011 01001001 01001001 01000011
01000001 00100000 01000100 01000101 00100000 01000100 01010010 01000101 01000011 01000101 00100000 01001001
01000001 01000011 01001001 11000011 10010011 01001110 00100000 01001101 01010100 01001110 01000100 01001001
01000001 01001100 01000001 00100000 01001001 01001110 01010100 01001001 01000101 01001100 01001001 00100000
01000011 01001001 01000001 00100000 01000100 01010101 01010010 01000101 01010010 01010100 01000001 01010100
01010101 01000001 01000100 00100000 01001001 01001110 01000111 01010011 01000101 01001110 01001001 01000001
01110010 01100101 01100001 01101100 01101001 01110011 01101101 01101111 00100000 01100101 01101110 00100000
01101100 01100001 01110011 00100000 01100011 01101111 01101101 01110000 01110101 01110100 01100001 01100100
01101111 01110010 01100001 01110011 00100000 01110010 01100101 01100001 01101100 00100000 01111001 00100000
01100100 01100101 00100000 01110000 01110010 01101111 01100011 01100101 01110011 01100001 01110010 00100000
01100100 00100000 01100100 01100101 00100000 01100100 01100001 01110100 01101111 01110011 00100000 00100000
```

This binary language allows computers to store and process vast amounts of data efficiently.

However, classical bits have a fundamental limitation: they can only exist in one state at a time either 0 or 1, but never both simultaneously. This restriction defines the capabilities of classical computers, making them fast but inherently limited in solving certain complex computational problems.

Unlike classical computers, quantum computers operate on an entirely different principle. Instead of classical bits, they use a special type of information unit called **quantum bits, or qubits**.

A qubit, like a classical bit, can represent **0** or **1**. However, what makes qubits extraordinary is their ability to exist in both states at the same time a property known as superposition.

But how does this happen? The answer lies in quantum mechanics, which governs the behavior of particles at the smallest scales. In quantum computing, the **spin** of a quantum particle determines its state:

Up spin (↑) corresponds to 1
Down spin (↓) corresponds to 0

50

However, due to the phenomenon of superposition, a qubit is not limited to just one of these states. Instead, it can exist in both 0 and 1 simultaneously until it is measured.

To better understand superposition, let's consider an everyday example: tossing a coin.

When you toss a coin, it can land on heads or tails just like a classical bit that can be either 0 or 1.

However, while the coin is in the air, it is spinning rapidly, and until it lands, we cannot say for sure whether it will be heads or tails.

Mathematically, during its flight, the coin is considered to be in a mixture of both heads and tails simultaneously. This uncertainty reflects the same principle as a qubit in superposition where it remains in both states (0 and 1) until it is measured.

In the case of quantum computing, this property of superposition allows qubits to perform multiple calculations at the same time, massively increasing computational power compared to classical computers.

In a classical computer, if you have 2 bits, they can represent only one state at a time (either 00, 01, 10, or 11).

However, in a quantum computer, 2 qubits in superposition can represent all four states (00, 01, 10, and 11) simultaneously.

If you scale this up to n qubits, they can process 2^n states at once.

This exponential growth in computational capacity makes quantum computers incredibly powerful for solving complex problems.

Understanding Real Power of Quantum Computing

Imagine you are in a massive library, but this isn't just any library. It has millions of books, and only one of them contains the exact information you need. The challenge? The books are not organized alphabetically, and you have no index to help you. If you were a classical computer, you would have no choice but to check each book one by one until you find the correct one. This process could take a long time, depending on the number of books.

However, a quantum computer functions differently. Instead of opening books one at a time, it has a special ability it can open multiple books simultaneously. How? Because of a quantum property called superposition, which allows it to exist in multiple states at the same time. While a classical bit in a computer can only be either 0 or 1, a quantum bit (qubit) can be both 0 and 1 at the same time.

Let's break it down further. In a classical computer:

If you have one bit, it can hold only one value (0 or 1) at a time.

If you have two bits, they can represent one of four possible states at any moment: 00, 01, 10, or 11 but only one of these at a time.

To check all possibilities, a classical computer must process each state sequentially.

But with quantum computing, a system with two qubits doesn't have to pick just one state. Thanks to superposition, it can exist in all four states at once: 00, 01, 10, and 11.

Now, imagine you increase the number of qubits:

3 qubits can exist in 8 states simultaneously.
4 qubits can exist in 16 states simultaneously.
100 qubits can exist in 2^{100} states at once, which is 1.26
nonillion states a number so large it surpasses the total
number of atoms in the observable universe.

This exponential growth in processing power is what makes
quantum computers so powerful. Instead of searching for
information one step at a time, they can analyze an enormous
number of possibilities simultaneously.

Now, you might wonder if a quantum computer explores
multiple possibilities at once, how does it determine the
correct one? After all, simply having a vast number of
potential answers isn't enough; we need a way to filter out the
wrong answers and identify the right one. This is where
quantum interference comes into play.

To understand quantum interference, let's return to our
library analogy. Imagine that we are searching for a book
containing the correct answer to a difficult question. A
classical computer would check each book one by one,
flipping through pages to verify whether it holds the answer.
This is a slow and methodical process.

However, a quantum computer behaves differently. Instead
of checking each book sequentially, imagine that every book
in the library sends out a unique signal or wave. But here's
the twist only the book with the correct answer sends a signal
that reinforces itself, while all the other books send signals
that cancel each other out.

This effect is known as **quantum interference**, and it is
crucial in how quantum computers process information. The
idea is that correct solutions interfere constructively
(amplifying their probability), while incorrect solutions
interfere destructively (reducing their probability). This
interference pattern naturally steers the quantum computer

toward the right answer without having to check each possibility individually.

The concept of quantum interference was famously explored by the legendary physicist Richard Feynman. He realized that in the quantum world, particles do not simply travel in a straight line from point A to point B. Instead, they behave in an incredibly strange and counterintuitive way:

A classical object, like a thrown baseball, follows a single, well-defined trajectory.

A quantum particle, such as an electron, doesn't just take one path it simultaneously explores every possible path between point A and point B.

At first, this might sound impossible, but experiments (such as the double-slit experiment) have confirmed that particles behave in this way. However, the key point is that not all paths contribute equally. Due to constructive and destructive interference, certain paths become more probable, and the particle ultimately follows the most efficient path.

This is remarkably similar to how a quantum computer works. Instead of considering all possible solutions equally, it leverages interference to enhance the correct answer while suppressing the incorrect ones.

Feynman took this idea a step further and mathematically formalized it into what is now called the Path Integral formulation of quantum mechanics. His work demonstrated that:

A quantum system does not take a single path but instead considers all possible paths simultaneously. The final behavior of the system is determined by interference paths that reinforce each other contribute more, while others cancel out. As a result, nature prefers the most efficient path, leading to an optimal outcome.

This principle is not just a theoretical concept it is one of the most fundamental rules governing the entire universe. From the behavior of tiny subatomic particles to large-scale phenomena like black holes, the Path Integral formulation plays a crucial role in understanding reality.

The reason quantum computing is so powerful is that it takes advantage of this natural tendency for quantum systems to find optimal solutions. Unlike classical computers, which must manually test each possibility, a quantum computer harnesses interference to amplify the correct answer and eliminate incorrect ones.

This means that for certain types of problems such as searching vast databases, solving complex equations, or optimizing logistics a quantum computer can arrive at the correct solution exponentially faster than any classical machine ever could.

We have now understood how quantum computers utilize superposition for parallel computing. Now, let's explore another powerful principle **quantum entanglement** and understand how computers harness its potential.

Quantum entanglement is a special connection between two particles where their states are linked, no matter how far apart they are. If you change something about one particle, the other particle instantly reacts, even if they are light-years away.

This is one of the most mind-blowing discoveries in quantum mechanics because it challenges our everyday understanding of physics. Normally, if you want to send information, you need something physical, like sound waves, electrical signals, or even light. But in quantum entanglement, no physical signal is sent, yet the two particles remain connected.

This phenomenon was first noticed by Albert Einstein, Boris Podolsky, and Nathan Rosen in 1935, leading to the famous **EPR Paradox**. Einstein even called it **"spooky action at a distance"** because it seemed to break the rules of classical physics.

Imagine you're solving a difficult puzzle, and instead of working on it alone, you have a magical connection with your friend. The moment you place one piece, your friend's piece automatically falls into place on the other side. This instant coordination allows you to solve the puzzle much faster than if you were working separately.

This is exactly how quantum entanglement helps in quantum computers. It allows quantum bits (qubits) to work together in a way that classical bits never could, making quantum computers incredibly powerful.

Point to be noticed: You cannot transfer classical information (like text, images, or messages) using quantum entanglement because of the limits set by **special relativity**.

Even though entangled particles affect each other instantly, the outcome of their measurements is completely random. This means you cannot control the information being sent. Since special relativity says that no information can travel faster than the speed of light, entanglement cannot be used for faster-than-light communication.

In classical computers, data is transferred from one bit to another through physical connections (like wires or circuits).

In quantum computers, entangled qubits share information instantly without needing a physical link.

This enables quantum computers to solve complex problems much faster than classical computers.

Example:
Imagine a team working on a project. If they communicate by email (like classical bits), it takes time. But if they have a telepathic link (like entangled qubits), they can instantly share ideas, making them work much faster!

So, based on this principle, multiple qubits can essentially work together like a team, allowing calculations to be performed in parallel and at extremely high speeds.

Quantum Decoherence

Quantum computers are designed to solve problems such as searching for the correct key among billions of possible keys or quickly finding the factorial of a large 200-digit number.

Quantum computers are particularly useful in scenarios where we need to extract meaningful patterns from an extreme amount of data or simulate quantum systems like atoms and molecules to understand their properties. These types of problems require massive parallelism, which traditional computers struggle to handle efficiently.

However, quantum algorithms have not yet advanced to the point where they can perform all general computing tasks like a classical operating system. As of today, quantum computers are built to solve only a few highly specific problems. Gradually, we are increasing the number of quantum algorithms and machines, and one day, we may even be able to execute quantum processes at room temperature just like nature does.

For example, in nature, plants perform photosynthesis at room temperature by absorbing light and carbon dioxide and converting them into sugar. Photosynthesis is a quantum phenomenon, but we still do not fully understand how it occurs at room temperature. So far, we have only been able to conduct controlled quantum interactions at extremely low temperatures, close to -273°C (absolute zero).

This is why today's quantum computers function more like refrigerators than traditional computers. They rely on an inner dilution refrigerator.

where the quantum chip is located at the very bottom. The large pipes you see in these systems are used to pump helium or nitrogen down to the lowest levels, cooling the chip. The wires passing through these pipes carry microwave signals, which are ultimately relayed to a classical computer for processing.

When a quantum computer is turned on, it is placed inside a large cylindrical enclosure known as an **outer dilution refrigerator**. This enclosure protects the processor from external heat, electromagnetic radiation, and environmental disturbances. These factors are major threats to quantum processors because their biggest enemy is **quantum**

decoherence, which can disrupt delicate quantum states and render computations useless.

Quantum particles behave like waves, but as soon as they interact with another particle or energy, their wave function collapses. This means they lose their quantum properties, such as superposition and entanglement, and become a definite particle. As a result, their quantum behavior is no longer useful.

The same thing happens with qubits. The moment a qubit interacts with anything, its quantum state collapses this phenomenon is called **decoherence**. To prevent decoherence, quantum processors are kept at temperatures close to absolute zero, which is the lowest possible temperature in the universe.

Absolute zero represents a state with virtually no unnecessary motion or heat. The pipes you see are part of a cooling system that maintains this extremely cold environment for the quantum processor.

Quantum Error Correction (QEC).

But even after all this qubits remain active for only a few microseconds before they rapidly decohere. This brief period, during which qubits stay in superposition and maintain their coherence, is known as **coherence time**. It represents one of the most significant challenges in making quantum computers a practical reality. Major tech companies working on quantum computing, including Google, IBM, and others, have been striving to extend this coherence time, but progress has been slow and challenging.

However, Google's Willow chip has made a remarkable breakthrough in this area. It has surpassed all existing superconducting quantum computers by increasing the coherence time by five times.

Despite this achievement, the Willow chip's coherence time still stands at just 100 microseconds, which is only 0.1 milliseconds. This means that an individual qubit can remain stable and perform calculations for an extremely short duration before it collapses.

Now, this raises a fundamental question: If a single qubit collapses within 100 microseconds, how can Google's quantum computer claim to run calculations for up to five minutes?

The answer lies in an advanced technique that forms the backbone of practical quantum computing **Quantum Error Correction (QEC)**.

Quantum error correction is a technique designed to detect and fix errors caused by decoherence. Since qubits are fragile and highly susceptible to disturbances, they need constant correction to ensure computations remain accurate and uninterrupted.

Imagine this process like a relay race:

Each qubit performs a small fraction of the calculation within its brief coherence time. Before it collapses, it transfers its processed information to another qubit. This next qubit continues the calculation and relays it forward in the same manner. The process repeats, allowing the computation to proceed for extended periods, even though individual qubits only last a few microseconds.

For this to work, error correction must occur in real time. Given that a qubit's coherence time is 100 microseconds, the error correction process must take place within at least 10 microseconds to ensure that information is transferred correctly before any collapse occurs.

This presents another major challenge: Quantum mechanics states that directly measuring a qubit collapses its quantum state. If any physical interaction with a qubit causes it to lose its superposition, how can error correction be performed without destroying the quantum state?

This is where Quantum Error Correction (QEC) comes in a special technique that corrects these errors and allows quantum computers to process information accurately without collapsing the quantum state.

To understand how Quantum Error Correction (QEC) works, we first need to break down the two types of errors that occur in quantum systems:

1. Bit Flip Error: When Qubits Change Their Values

Imagine a classical computer where information is stored in bits tiny electrical signals that can be either 0 or 1. If a bit gets corrupted due to noise or interference, a 0 might accidentally turn into 1, or vice versa.

Similarly, in quantum computing, a bit flip error happens when a qubit, which should be $|0\rangle$, suddenly changes into $|1\rangle$, or a qubit in $|1\rangle$ state flips to $|0\rangle$.

Think of this as flipping a coin. If you originally have a coin showing heads (0), but an accidental disturbance flips it to tails (1), your information has changed. In quantum computing, this kind of error can lead to incorrect calculations.

2. Phase Flip Error: When the Quantum Relationship Changes

The second type of error, phase flip error, is more complex because it doesn't affect whether the qubit is $|0\rangle$ or $|1\rangle$, but instead changes the phase of the qubit's quantum state.

To understand this, recall that quantum computing is based on **superposition** meaning a qubit can exist in a blend of both $|0\rangle$ and $|1\rangle$ at the same time. This blend is represented as $|\psi\rangle = |0\rangle + |1\rangle$ (a superposition of both states).

However, if a phase flip error occurs, the qubit's state changes to $|0\rangle - |1\rangle$. Notice that the numbers remain the same, but the sign has changed (from + to -). This might seem like a small change, but it dramatically alters how the qubit interacts with other qubits, potentially leading to incorrect calculations.

How are these two errors fixed to understand this imagine you are building a sandcastle, but as soon as wind or water touches it, it starts to fall apart. To protect it, you must shield it from these elements but for how long can you keep it safe?

Quantum qubits face a similar challenge: they cannot interact with anything accidentally, or their delicate quantum state will be disturbed.

But what if, instead of protecting just one sandcastle, you build multiple identical replicas? Now, even if one sandcastle is damaged by wind or water, you can use the others as a reference to repair and restore the original structure.

This is exactly how quantum error correction works. It uses a technique called redundancy, where information is spread across multiple entangled qubits, ensuring that even if one qubit is affected by an error, the system can detect and correct it using the others.

In this technique, the information stored in a single logical qubit is encoded using three physical qubits. This means that instead of keeping the information in just one qubit, we distribute it across three qubits to make it more resilient to errors.

Instead of storing a logical qubit as just $|0\rangle$ or $|1\rangle$, we encode it as:

$|0\rangle \rightarrow |000\rangle$ (all three qubits in state 0)

$|1\rangle \rightarrow |111\rangle$ (all three qubits in state 1)

Mathematically, any quantum state:

$|\psi\rangle = a|0\rangle + b|1\rangle$

is stored as:

$|\psi\rangle = a|000\rangle + b|111\rangle$

This ensures that even if one of the qubits experiences an error, we can still recover the correct information.

Let's say one of the qubits flips accidentally for example, a 0 changes to 1:

$a|100\rangle + b|011\rangle$

Now, the information is corrupted, but since we have extra qubits, we can detect and fix this error.

To correct the error, special helper qubits called ancilla qubits are used.

Quantum gates are used to deploy certain helper qubits, also known as ancilla qubits, which become entangled with potential errors in the system.

Just like logical gates in a classical circuit direct the flow of electrons to perform logical operations, quantum logic gates control the state and evolution of quantum particles (qubits) in a structured manner. These ancilla qubits, being quantum particles themselves, can interact with computational qubits that may contain errors, allowing error information to be extracted without disturbing the computation itself.

When we measure these ancilla qubits, their quantum state collapses, revealing the presence and nature of the error (e.g., bit-flip or phase-flip errors). The key advantage of this technique is that the logical quantum system remains undisturbed, as we do not directly measure or interfere with the qubits performing computations. Instead, we only interact with the ancilla qubits, which were entangled with the computational qubits, and extract error information indirectly.

Once the error is precisely identified, it can be corrected using quantum logic gates. These gates apply appropriate transformations (such as X gates for bit-flip correction or Z gates for phase-flip correction) to restore the correct state of the affected qubit. This process is cyclical and continuous, ensuring that quantum computations remain stable and free from accumulating errors.

The entire error detection and correction process is typically completed within a few microseconds (e.g., 10 microseconds in some implementations), making it extremely fast, efficient, and essential for fault-tolerant quantum computing.

In the case of phase-flip errors we create three copies, forming the quantum state $000 + 111$. Mathematically, this is represented as a $(+++) + b(---)$, where a and b are quantum probability amplitudes.

A special helper qubit scans the system to check for mismatches. Since qubits are entangled, errors on one qubit affect the entire system. If an error occurs (e.g., one qubit's phase flips from + to -), the helper qubit measures the difference and flags the problem. The helper qubit does not disturb the system but provides information about which qubit has flipped. This process is called syndrome measurement, similar to a security system detecting an intruder without stopping normal operations. Once the error is detected, quantum logic gates correct it by flipping the affected qubit back to its correct phase. This ensures that the quantum state remains stable and can continue functioning correctly.

Peter Shor's Breakthrough in Quantum Error Correction

A major advancement in error correction came from Peter Shor, a quantum scientist who developed a powerful error correction algorithm. His method protects against both bit-flip and phase-flip errors simultaneously, making quantum computations more reliable.

One fascinating aspect of quantum error correction is that it allows quantum computers to perform complex mathematical calculations, such as finding the factorial of large numbers or solving optimization problems.

Think of this like a relay race: if one runner falls, their teammates can pick up the baton and keep running. Similarly, quantum computers do not lose information permanently; they extract data from remaining qubits and continue calculations seamlessly.

Google's Willow Chip: A Major Breakthrough in Quantum Error Correction

Just like that, Google's Willow chip has also achieved a breakthrough result in its quantum error correction code.

Google recently made significant progress in quantum error correction with its Willow chip. This new quantum processor has achieved:

• An increased number of qubits, allowing more complex quantum operations.
• A lower error rate, making quantum computations more stable.

Despite these advancements, quantum computers are not yet practical for real-world applications. While companies like Google, IBM, and Honeywell are making breakthroughs, they have not yet built a quantum computer capable of solving real-life problems on a large scale. Challenges such as qubit stability, error rates, and scalability still need to be addressed before quantum computing becomes widely useful.

Quantum computers have the potential to revolutionize the world by solving problems that are impossible for classical computers. However, we are still far from making them useful for real-world applications. There are three major challenges that must be overcome:

1. **Stability of Quantum States**
2. **Effective Quantum Algorithms**
3. **Real-Time Error Correction**

1. Stability of Quantum States

One of the biggest challenges in quantum computing is keeping qubits stable. Qubits, the basic units of quantum computers, exist in a delicate state called superposition, where they can be both 0 and 1 at the same time. However, this state is extremely fragile.

Decoherence – Qubits lose their quantum state when they interact with their surroundings. This happens due to vibrations, temperature fluctuations, or electromagnetic interference.

Noise – Even the smallest disturbances can cause errors, making quantum computations unreliable.

Think of a qubit like a spinning coin. While it's spinning, it's in superposition it could land on heads or tails. But if you breathe on it, touch it, or even make a slight vibration, the coin will fall, collapsing into either heads or tails. This is similar to how qubits lose their quantum state due to decoherence.

To solve this, researchers are working on quantum error correction techniques and developing better materials that can keep qubits stable for longer.

2. Effective Quantum Algorithms

Even if we could build stable quantum computers, we need effective quantum algorithms to make use of their power. Unlike classical computers, which run step-by-step instructions, quantum computers operate differently, using principles like superposition and entanglement to process vast amounts of data simultaneously.

The Problem with Quantum Algorithms

Lack of General-Purpose Algorithms – We don't yet have enough practical algorithms to solve a wide range of problems.

Complexity – Writing quantum algorithms requires deep knowledge of quantum mechanics and mathematics, making them difficult to develop.

Imagine you have a super-fast car, but there's no road built for it. You can't use it effectively. Similarly, quantum computers need specialized algorithms to perform calculations that classical computers can't.

Scientists like Peter Shor and Lov Grover have developed some breakthrough quantum algorithms:

Shor's Algorithm can factorize large numbers exponentially faster than classical computers. This could break modern encryption methods.

Grover's Algorithm can search huge databases much faster, which could be useful for artificial intelligence and data science.

However, for quantum computers to be truly useful, researchers need to develop many more such algorithms for different real-world problems.

3. Real-Time Quantum Error Correction

Even if qubits were stable and we had powerful algorithms, errors in quantum computations are a major issue. Unlike classical computers, which use error-checking methods like parity bits, quantum computers need specialized quantum error correction techniques.

Why Do Errors Happen?

Qubits are extremely sensitive – Even a tiny environmental disturbance can cause errors.

Measurement Problem – Measuring a qubit destroys its quantum state, so we can't check for errors the way we do in classical computers.

Each of these problems is a massive roadblock, and solving them is not just a technical challenge it could change the future of computing in ways we can't even imagine today. Let's explore these changes in detail.

1. Quantum Computing in Drug Discovery

Imagine trying to unlock a door with a giant keychain that has millions or even billions of keys. The only way to find the right key is by testing each one one at a time until you finally find the one that fits. This is similar to how modern drug discovery works today it is a slow, expensive, and trial-and-error process. But quantum computing has the potential to change this completely, reducing a process that takes 15–20 years and billions of dollars into something that could happen in just a few months.

This breakthrough is possible because of how molecules behave at the atomic level, which follows the rules of quantum mechanics the same principles that quantum computers use.

Let's break this down step by step.

Every medicine is made of molecules that must interact with complex proteins in the human body.

There are billions of possible molecular combinations that could work.

Scientists must simulate and test these combinations, which takes enormous time and computing power.

Why Is This So Difficult?

The interactions between molecules and proteins involve complex quantum mechanical processes, meaning they are highly unpredictable.

Even the most powerful classical supercomputers can only approximate these interactions using 3D models.

This process is extremely resource-intensive, requiring years of research and billions of dollars before a new drug reaches the market.

Let's take an example:

When pharmaceutical companies were looking for a vaccine for COVID-19, they had to test millions of molecular structures to see which ones could trigger the right immune response.

Even with modern AI and supercomputers, this process still took several months to find effective candidates.

If quantum computers were available, they could have simulated and analyzed these molecules much faster, potentially reducing the time to weeks or even days.

2. The Key to Ending Pandemics Forever

Throughout history, epidemics and pandemics have been among the biggest threats to human civilization. From the Black Death in the 14th century, which wiped out over 50 million people, to the Spanish Flu in 1918, which killed tens of millions, and even the COVID-19 pandemic, which paralyzed the world infectious diseases have repeatedly changed the course of history.

But what if we could eliminate pandemics forever?

With quantum computing, we may finally have the power to predict and stop deadly viruses before they spread, ensuring that outbreaks never reach a tipping point. Instead of reacting after a pandemic has already begun, we could prevent it entirely.

Let's break down how this would work.

Understanding How Viruses and Pathogens Spread

To stop pandemics, we first need to understand how viruses spread and evolve.

Viruses mutate rapidly – This means their genetic structure keeps changing, which makes it hard to create long-lasting vaccines.

Deadly mutations happen randomly – Scientists struggle to predict which mutations will make a virus more dangerous.

Finding a cure takes too long – Even with advanced computing, it can take months or even years to develop vaccines and treatments.

Take COVID-19, for example:

The virus mutated multiple times, leading to variants like Delta and Omicron, making it harder to control.

Scientists had to study millions of samples, trying to predict which variants would become dangerous.

Even though vaccines were developed quickly compared to past diseases, it still took months, allowing the virus to spread globally.

With quantum computing, all of this could change.

How Quantum Computing Can Stop Pandemics Before They Start

1. Predicting Deadly Mutations Before They Happen

Viruses mutate at the molecular level, meaning their genetic codes change in ways that are difficult to track.

A quantum computer can analyze every possible mutation at once, predicting which ones are likely to become dangerous.

This means scientists can identify high-risk variants before they spread, allowing us to act before a pandemic starts.

Real-World Impact:

Instead of waiting for a new virus strain to appear and cause panic, governments and health organizations could start preparing months or years in advance.

If quantum computers had been available before COVID-19, they could have predicted the emergence of dangerous mutations like Delta and Omicron before they spread globally.

2. Developing Vaccines in Weeks Instead of Years

Today, vaccine development is a slow and expensive process that requires:

- **Identifying the virus structure**
- **Testing different compounds**
- **Running long clinical trials**

Quantum computers can simulate virus-protein interactions instantly, finding the perfect vaccine formula in weeks instead of years.

Example:

When the COVID-19 vaccine was developed, researchers had to test millions of possible molecular structures to see which would trigger an immune response.

Quantum computing could have analyzed all possible vaccine combinations simultaneously, reducing vaccine development time from months to days.

This means that for future pandemics, we won't need to shut down economies or go into lockdowns we could have a working vaccine ready within weeks.

3. Stopping Viruses Before They Reach the Tipping Point

Every pandemic begins as a small outbreak, which grows exponentially.

If we can identify dangerous pathogens early, we can prevent them from ever spreading globally.

How This Works in Real Life:

Governments could track and contain outbreaks in real-time, stopping them before they spread worldwide.

Instead of reacting after a disease has killed millions, we could stop it at the source

3. Treatment for Incurable Diseases

Right now, many of the most devastating diseases have no cure. Why? Because they are caused by protein malfunctions inside the body an area of science that is extremely difficult to understand and predict. However, quantum computers have the potential to decode these complex biological processes, leading to revolutionary medical advancements.

Let's break it down step by step.

Why Do So Many Diseases Have No Cure?

Most life-threatening diseases, such as cancer, Alzheimer's, and Parkinson's, are caused by problems at the molecular level specifically by proteins folding incorrectly inside the body.

What Are Proteins

Proteins are the building blocks of life. Every function in our body from digesting food to fighting infections is controlled by proteins.

But proteins don't just exist as straight chains of molecules. They must fold into complex 3D shapes to work properly. If this folding process goes wrong, serious diseases can occur.

Example - Cancer

Cancer is caused by mutations that change how proteins fold, leading to uncontrolled cell growth.

If we could accurately predict and fix faulty protein folding, we could stop cancer before it even starts.

The problem? Simulating protein folding is incredibly difficult.

The Challenge of Simulating Protein Folding

Understanding how proteins fold requires us to simulate every possible shape they can take. This is like trying to solve a gigantic 3D puzzle with millions of pieces.

Proteins are made up of thousands of atoms, and each atom interacts with the others in complex ways.

Even the most powerful classical supercomputers today struggle to simulate a single protein because the calculations are too complex.

The process takes years, making drug discovery slow and expensive.

Example:

Right now, scientists use trial and error to develop new drugs. They test millions of chemical compounds to see which ones might work.

This process can take 10–20 years and cost billions of dollars.

But quantum computers could solve this problem in just weeks or months.

How Quantum Computing Will Revolutionize Medicine

Quantum computers do not calculate like normal computers. Instead of solving one possibility at a time, they can analyze all possible protein foldings at once.

Scientists will no longer have to **guess and check** new medicines.

Quantum computers will instantly analyze which drugs will work against diseases like cancer and Alzheimer's.

Instead of waiting decades for a cure, we could find it in just weeks or months.

Personalized Medicine

Right now, everyone gets the same type of medicine, even though people's bodies react differently.

Quantum computers will allow doctors to analyze a person's unique DNA and create customized treatments that work specifically for them.

4. Unlocking the Secrets of Space

Space has always been the ultimate mystery filled with black holes, dark matter, and the possibility of alien life. But today, even with the most powerful supercomputers, we struggle to understand the universe's deepest secrets.

Quantum computing is about to change everything.

Since the universe itself operates on quantum laws, quantum computers will allow us to model space with incredible accuracy. This will lead to huge breakthroughs in space exploration, spacecraft technology, and even the discovery of extraterrestrial life.

Let's explore how.

1. Unlocking the Mysteries of Black Holes and Dark Matter

For decades, scientists have struggled to fully understand black holes and quantum gravity. These are some of the most complex phenomena in physics because they involve both relativity and quantum mechanics two theories that do not currently work together.

How Quantum Computing Will Help:

Quantum computers can simulate black hole physics more accurately than ever before.

They can help us understand how information behaves inside a black hole.

They could even provide insights into the nature of space-time itself.

Solving the Mystery of Dark Matter & Dark Energy

Dark matter makes up 85% of the universe, yet we cannot see it or directly detect it.

Dark energy is driving the expansion of the universe, but we don't know how it works.

Today's computers cannot handle the calculations needed to truly understand them, but quantum computers might crack the code.

What If We Could Control These Forces?

If we understand dark matter and dark energy, we might one day use them to create futuristic technologies.

Imagine spaceships powered by dark energy, allowing us to travel across galaxies at incredible speeds!

2. Mastering Space Navigation

Right now, sending a spacecraft to Mars requires solving millions of equations to predict its path, avoid obstacles, and land safely.

But what if we could calculate space trajectories instantly and with perfect accuracy?

Quantum Computing Will Allow Us To:

Predict the motion of every planet, star, and asteroid in real-time.

Avoid space debris and navigate through dangerous regions of the galaxy.

Make long-distance space travel safer and faster.

The Future of Space Travel

Colonizing Mars and other planets would become easier and more efficient.

We could explore exoplanets outside our solar system with extreme precision.

3. Developing Advanced Spacecraft & Rocket Materials

To explore deep space, we need stronger, lighter, and more efficient spacecraft. Right now, designing a new rocket takes years of research and expensive trial and error.

How Quantum Computers Will Change This:

Build stronger and heat-resistant spaceships.
Improve fuel efficiency, making space travel cheaper and faster.

Design spacecraft that can withstand the harshest conditions of space.

Example:

Quantum simulations could create materials stronger than steel but lighter than aluminum, perfect for building advanced space colonies.

We could develop self-repairing spacecraft that can fix themselves in deep space.

4. Finding Alien Life Will Become Easier

Right now, scientists at SETI (Search for Extraterrestrial Intelligence) are scanning space for radio signals from alien civilizations. But after more than 20 years of searching, we have found nothing.

Why?

Space is filled with noise radio waves from stars, galaxies, and cosmic phenomena.

We have to filter out real alien signals from millions of random signals an impossible task for today's computers.

How Quantum Computing Will Help:

Analyze and filter trillions of space signals in seconds.

Separate intelligent alien signals from background noise with perfect accuracy.

Process massive planetary data sets to detect possible bio-signatures of life.

What Else Quantum Computing Can Do?

Using Drake's Equation, we can scan thousands of exoplanets and instantly identify planets most likely to have life.

Quantum computers will help us detect atmospheric signatures (like oxygen and methane) on distant planets, which are strong indicators of life.

With quantum computing, we might detect alien life within our lifetime either through signals or by identifying planets with the right conditions for life

5. The Future of Physics and Mathematics

The world of physics and mathematics is about to undergo a massive transformation. Today, some of the most complex equations in quantum mechanics, relativity, and theoretical physics take years or even decades to solve. But with quantum computing, these problems will be solved in seconds, unlocking new technologies and discoveries at an exponential rate.

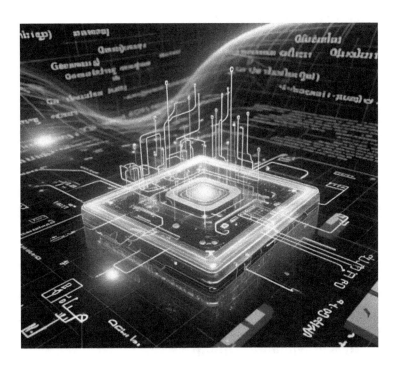

1. Solving the Most Complex Equations Instantly

Right now, some equations in quantum mechanics, string theory, and general relativity are so complex that even the most powerful supercomputers struggle to solve them.

But quantum computers which operate on qubits instead of binary bits will allow us to:

Solve multi-variable differential equations in quantum physics.

Model gravitational waves, wormholes, and time dilation effects.

Simulate multi-particle quantum interactions that are currently impossible to study.

2. A New Era of Mathematical Discoveries

Mathematics is the foundation of every technology we use today. However, certain areas of math, such as chaos theory, prime number distribution, and topology, are still not fully understood.

Quantum Computers Will Help Us:

Solve the most complex mathematical proofs instantly.

Predict patterns in nature, weather, and economics with near-perfect accuracy.

Unlock new fields of quantum geometry and higher-dimensional mathematics.

Breakthrough Possibilities:

Solving the Riemann Hypothesis, a 150-year-old mystery about prime numbers.

Understanding the mathematics of black holes at a deeper level.

Creating ultra-secure cryptographic systems that no hacker can break.

6. Artificial Intelligence (AI) and Quantum Computing.

If there are two technologies destined to merge, it's Artificial Intelligence (AI) and Quantum Computing. They are like long-lost brothers, meant to work together to push human civilization into an unimaginable future.

Quantum computers can process massive amounts of data exponentially faster, while AI can learn and adapt like a human brain. When combined, these two forces could create a self-sustaining loop of continuous improvement:

- Quantum computers will accelerate AI learning, allowing AI **to** think, process, and evolve at unimaginable speeds.
- AI will design better quantum hardware, making quantum computers more powerful and efficient.
- This loop will keep going forever each improving the other exponentially.

And It Will NEVER Stop!

This means that human civilization could advance at an infinite rate, possibly reaching Type 2 or Type 3 on the Kardashev Scale much sooner than we think!

From an Earth-Bound Civilization to a Galactic Empire?

Today, when we talk about Type 2 or Type 3 civilizations, it feels like a distant dream an impossible reality. But the moment we fully harness quantum computing and AI, suddenly, it doesn't seem so far-fetched anymore.

What's Next? The Birth of the Ultimate AI

Once AI and Quantum Computing fully merge, we might see:

AI-powered scientists discovering breakthroughs at lightning speed.

Super intelligent AI designing entire cities, industries, and even governing civilizations.

Digital immortality uploading human consciousness into quantum neural networks.

Maybe we won't just explore the universe… we'll become something greater than we ever imagined.

Are we on the edge of something much bigger than humanity itself?

References

https://historified.in/2024/04/16/decoding-the-antikythera-mechanism-unraveling-the-secrets-of-ancient-technology/

https://en.wikipedia.org/wiki/Antikythera_mechanism#:~:text=The%20Antikythera%20mechanism%20(/,and%20worked.%5B20%5D

https://www.nature.com/articles/s41598-021-84310-w#:~:text=Reconstructing%20the%20Cosmos%20at%20the,in%20Supplementary%20Discussion%20S2.

https://www.sciencemuseum.org.uk/objects-and-stories/charles-babbages-difference-engines-and-science-museum#:~:text=Example%20of%20a,Science%20%20Museum%20Group

https://www.wowstem.org/post/ada-lovelace#:~:text=This%20one%20was,really%20clever%20idea!

https://en.wikipedia.org/wiki/Note_G#:~:text=In%20the%20modern%20era%2C%20thanks,to%20a%20minor%20typographical%20error.

https://en.wikipedia.org/wiki/History_of_the_tran
sistor#:~:text=The%20Bell%20team%20made,t
ransistor%20had%20been%20invented.

https://engineerguy.com/making/background-
transistor-
operation.pdf?utm_source=chatgpt.com

https://www.intel.com/content/www/us/en/newsr
oom/tech101/the-transistor-
explained.html#gs.j64res:~:text=How%20the%
20Modern,of%20the%20universe.

https://www.waferworld.com/post/how-small-
can-transistors-
get#:~:text=How%20Big%20Is%20the%20Typi
cal,point%20are%20sub%2D100%20nanomete
rs.

https://www.investopedia.com/terms/m/mooresl
aw.asp#:~:text=secondsVolume%200%25-
,What%20Is%20Moore%27s%20Law%3F,was
%20an%20observation%20and%20extrapolatio
n%20that%20has%20held%20steady%20since
%201965.,-KEY%20TAKEAWAYS

https://en.wikipedia.org/wiki/Transistor_count#Microprocessors:~:text=Plot%20of%20MOS%20transistor%20counts%20for%20microprocessors%20against%20dates%20of%20in%C2%ADtro%C2%ADduction.%20The%20curve%20shows%20counts%20doubling%20every%20two%20years%2C%20per%20Moore%27s%20law.

https://www.britannica.com/technology/Pascaline#:~:text=Pascaline%2C%20the%20first,next%2010%20years.

https://en.wikipedia.org/wiki/Thermionic_emission#:~:text=This%20effect%20had,%5B23%5D

https://www.forbes.com/sites/ibm/2016/05/04/with-the-dawn-of-quantum-computing-lets-build-a-quantum-community/#:~:text=In%201981%2C%20at,look%20so%20easy.%22

https://builtin.com/hardware/quantum-computing-applications#:~:text=10%20Quantum%20Computing%20Applications%20to,new%20era%20in%20quantum%20computing.

https://pixelplex.io/blog/quantum-computing-applications/

https://www.quantum-machines.co/blog/understanding-googles-quantum-error-correction-breakthrough/#:~:text=At%20the%20heart%20of%20the%20system%20was%20real%2Dtime%20synchronization.%20Every%20correction%20cycle%20had%20to%20complete%20within%201.1%20%C2%B5s%E2%80%94a%20narrow%20window%20in%20which%20the%20qubits%20were%20measured

Image Credits

- National Archaeological Museum, Athens, Greece, by Tilemahos Efthimiadis]. Licensed under Creative Commons Attribution 2.0 Generic. Retrieved from https://www.flickr.com/photos/telemax/3471171927/
- Antikythera mechanism used to calculate astronomical positions, by Magnus Hagdorn. Licensed under Creative Commons Attribution-Share Alike 2.0 Generic. Retrieved from https://www.flickr.com/photos/hagdorned/7751351552/
- **Français :** Machine arithmétique de Pascal, 1642, by Miniwark. Licensed under Creative Commons Attribution-Share Alike 4.0 International. Retrieved from https://commons.wikimedia.org/wiki/File:Machine_arithm%C3%A9tique_de_Pascal,_1642.jpg
- Calculator constructed by Gottfried Wilhelm Leibniz, by Hannes Grobe. Licensed under the Creative Commons Attribution 3.0 Unported. Retrieved from https://commons.m.wikimedia.org/wiki/File:Leibniz-Rechenmaschine_hg.jpg
- A photo of the Difference Engine constructed by the Science Museum based on the plans for Charles Babbage's Difference Engine No. 2, by User:Geni. Licensed under the **Creative Commons** Attribution-Share Alike **4.0 International**, **3.0 Unported**, **2.5 Generic**, **2.0 Generic** and **1.0 Generic.** Retrieved from https://commons.wikimedia.org/wiki/User:Geni

- Babbage's Analytical Engine, by Mrjohncummings. Licensed under the Creative Commons Attribution-Share Alike 2.0 Generic. Retrieved from https://commons.wikimedia.org/wiki/User:Mrjohncummings
- Thomas Edison, by Wikipedia. Licensed under the Creative Commons Attribution-Share Alike 4.0 International. Retrieved from https://en.wikipedia.org/wiki/War_of_the_currents
- Vacuum tube computing, by Kanagawa, Japan. Licensed under the Creative Commons Attribution 2.0 Generic. Retrieved from https://www.flickr.com/photos/monchan/30781535612/
- The first transistor ever made, built by John Bardeen, William Shockley and Walter H. Brattain of Bell Labs in 1947, by Unitronic. Licensed under the Creative Commons Attribution-Share Alike 3.0 Unported. Retrieved from https://commons.wikimedia.org/wiki/File:1st-Transistor.jpg
- Replica of first integrated circuit by Jack Kilby, by Florian Schäffer. Licensed under the Creative Commons Attribution-Share Alike 4.0 International. Retrieved from https://commons.wikimedia.org/wiki/File:Replica_IC.png
- A processor Intel C4004, by Thomas Nguyen. Licensed under the Creative Commons Attribution-Share Alike 4.0 International. Retrieved from https://stelo.xyz/Museum/4004/

- An illustration of the 'Double-slit experiment' in physics, by NekoJaNekoJa. Licensed under the Creative Commons Attribution-Share Alike 4.0 Internationa. Retrieved from https://commons.wikimedia.org/wiki/File:Double-slit.PNG
- Binary code matrix, by Graph+sas. Licensed under the Creative Commons Attribution-Share Alike 4.0 International. Retrieved from https://commons.wikimedia.org/wiki/File:Binary-code.png
- Today's quantum computer, by Steve Jurvetson. Licensed under the Creative Commons Attribution 2.0 Generic. Retrieved from https://www.flickr.com/photos/jurvetson/3796519198/

Congratulations on reaching the end of *Classical to Quantum: A Complete Guide to the Evolution of Computers!* I hope this journey through the history and future of computing has been insightful.

Your opinion matters! If you enjoyed this book or found it useful, please consider leaving a review. Your feedback helps improve future editions and guides new readers in their learning journey.

Thank you for your time and support!

Naveen Patidar

www.ingramcontent.com/pod-product-compliance
Lightning Source LLC
La Vergne TN
LVHW052307060326
832902LV00021B/3755